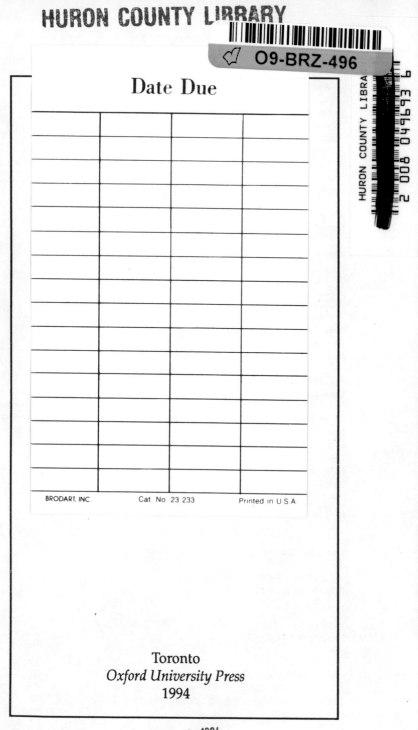
Date Due

BRODART, INC.   Cat. No. 23 233   Printed in U.S.A.

Toronto
Oxford University Press
1994

Oxford University Press
70 Wynford Drive, Don Mills, Ontario M3C 1J9

Oxford New York
Athens Auckland Bangkok Bombay
Calcutta Cape Town Dar es Salaam Delhi
Florence Hong Kong Istanbul Karachi
Kuala Lumpur Madras Madrid Melbourne
Mexico City Nairobi Paris Singapore
Taipei Tokyo Toronto

and associated companies in
Berlin Ibadan

Oxford is a trademark of Oxford University Press

ACKNOWLEDGEMENTS
The author wishes to thank Brian Henderson for his dedication and kindness. His vision of this book as part of a series of "Selected"s tempted the manuscript out of me, and encouraged the approbation of my publishers, House of Anansi and Véhicule Press.

AUTHOR'S NOTE
Concerning the work from *Furious* (Anansi, 1988, reprinted 1993):
Because excerpting from *Furious* obliterates the design in which the poems are meant to appear, a note is in order. *Furious* consists of two parts, poems and a prose section or meditation called "The Acts"; together they form a kind of lattice. In the full book, the points of contact between individual "acts" and poems are indicated only by footnote numbers in the table of contents. In the excerpts printed here, footnote numbers are also marked next to the poem titles in the text, even when the "act" toward which the poem beckons is not present.

P.S. I have talked to my aunt since.

Canadian Cataloguing in Publication Data
Mouré, Erin, 1955-
    The green word: selected poems
    ISBN 0-19-541077-7
    I. Title.
    PS8576.096A6 1994   C811'.54   C94-931900-7
    PR9199.3.M68A6 1994

THE GREEN WORD

✧ **from *Empire, York Street***

HAZARD OF THE OCCUPATION

what is said about the earth is
only that it breaks
apart. the child severed
from one arm in a laundromat
is sutured to the limb; it refuses to
belong: does he know where his arm
goes?
this is how easily a man breaks apart.
flesh as thin as words.

in the morning, your muscles ache from
the places they go in the night.
tho you argue, they will not
raise you from the bed.
you cannot forsake your arms.
outside, a hummingbird refuses to
land on the roof.
shingles break apart,
the hummingbird spins its wings above.
there is no word for what happens.

the table breaks when you lay your hands
upon it, splinters thru the floor.
facts, too; they do not remain fact.
on the page, words rearrange,
accuse you, shout about abuse.
the hummingbird lands.

your legs glare from the corner, accusing
you of theft; they want
divorce, requital, an argument over particulars.
pages hum; presses are
bolted into guns.
this time you remember nothing.
your legs dodge down
the road, sick w/ explosions:
in the throat, the word
ascends; its wings break
against your tongue

MIDWAY, 10 YEARS AGO

where her life went, no one knew.
she followed it just half-way, stopped, & screamed
something about a nervous breakdown.
enough of grieving children, & neighbours
w/ their rancorous tongues.
enough of wisdom, & words, & days
sapped by the old arrangement.
what she cherished was past: chance
mortality stole it. His laughter, its sound
suspended, & the wet aroma of trees.
talk of completion, the unmarked years.
ah, the boy w/ the beat-up Volvo is gone now,
& won't be coming back for Easter, or for ever.
his apparition sleeps grey-haired on the sofa
when the meal's over.
                                less & less
to say, to revoke.
She can't tell him of the voices,
or when she wakes, how the word catches her
half-way out of the room, & she listens,
walls & ceilings bent around.
familiar objects muddle at her touch, turn away.
neither will the bruised air assure her.
alone, days of the week
hunt her cunningly, sit & laugh thru their tortured faces.
she won't recognize her children now.
                                        it's this point, here,
where she stopped. the sudden flame of her heart
shuttered.
so.
when the doctor came, he said she had ruined
herself, & he led her to the taxi, talking
of solace, of what reason there is

TRESPASS

Outside, the sun tries on one tree after another.
So many spent clothes, last
year's boots left by the garage-door step
as warning.
The tired race of ideas swarms around the head,
is sheltered by curious brown hair, irregular.
As i say: swarms like gnats grown fat & unkempt
on a raw diet.
The sun picks out the garage roof, corrugated iron
wrappt like a cloak.
O child in the brown coat, wearing out the gravel
w/ your song, tell us, compel us
like the haze as the sun eats it hugely, that we too
should carry, a rapture
beneficent, benedictory, as trees
bear their shook leaves.
Those gnats are ideas, forgotten the meaning of prayer.
What is it the words tell over, over?
Their metaphor too primitive
to unlock the wide boat of memory.

My grandfather was a stern man, his house now a chicken coop;
his sons built another & stayed
at a hotel in town when it burst, flaming.
Soon enough.
Trespass with 4 s's or none is still trespass.
There is only one of everything, includes the crimes.
I want to know perfectly
how much arm is exacted in penalty.
I will go myself to tell him; he said
finally one waits alone.
After the sun goes,
i too, wearing the old boots & no wonder!

EPIPHANY

1

When the man hiked down w/ perfect
blood in his mouth, coughing, his hands
bearing white syllables like sores: able
to iterate image from the blockt building;
w/ the exact beatitude of knives.
Like the flushing of an artery, this
the civilized call distasteful, & turn.
The building is, true enough,
difficult to inhabit. Highways w/ their shorn cliffs
leading into the high passes
make no consolation, no warning.
The bleakness you see is the swell
of your own heart in front of you, spectator.
This landscape is only as good
as the moment your hand reaches out to the man; now
accept his gift of syllables, if you believe
it can kill you

2

Everywhere brown-lipped glaciers receding:
geologists hone their picks, measure the rock w/ its
faults & collapses.
Its volcanic intrusion, slip, geologic age.
Just try & breathe around it.

Cameras record the geologist, standing; his picture
placed in a book, written:
                    The principal industries were Forests & Mines.
That year Mr Minister told in the papers
he would spray the chemical from planes
on his children, to save them
from budworm.
Because. When the trees die, the governed
are depleted, agencies of the poor are measured

(no stanza break)

gainst the corporation & found wanting.
They are all wanting.
Blessed are the meek, they shall inherit
syllables, a handful.
So much for platitude; those who mock
ascend the ladder of political beauty, talk
of austerity.
Dispel your own disease.
Frankly, the man holding all those syllables is too crazy.
Beware of them. How could they be graces.

14.08.77/Golden, BC

JUBILARE

> ...but in the end you will be guided not
> by what it would be practically helpful to learn,
> but by what it is possible to learn.
> > J. Robert Oppenheimer

> The ones who have had a fatal accident, and all
> those who have not...
> > Lina Wertmüller

Finally there is no amnesty; little more
than a lens-cap, broken flashcube,
a house made out of twine.
today the evangelists have reached Trafalgar Square:
one man w/ a trombone marks their Front, below
the tourists sing *glory glory glory*;
all exit blocked in the rush of hands.

Above the square in the gallery hangs
Ingres' head of Pindar; the face
of one who has abandoned hope
who is also the victor,
triumphant, holder of the prize.
he accepts the laurels, knowing
the Front can never reach him;
his own praise borne willingly, always,
for even the place where he stands is not far
from the sound of tears, one hammer
away.

In the square, still
they push open their throats for amnesty.
pigeons have fled.
the underground is full of everyone
you know, thick-fisted w/ telephone number, lottery numbers,
signed cheques w/ scenes
of Canada in Four Seasons.
they are preparing to rise in one chorus, holding
the Writ to a new order.
some of us will be left behind, they say.
do you love your factory? they ask.

Above them, a man lifts his trombone & laughs.
he knows of a justice that makes the guilty innocent, & frees them.
he knows there is no realism in art.
he believes he will never be prime minister.
he is barely loved.
yes, there are allegiances that forgive us, if we speak their name.
& permit us, later, w/ guns or cabbages.
it is because the word is rescue, & possible,
that we sit in the torn wood & sing that line:
w/ failed measure, poor habits, longing
to dwell here –

12.06.77/London

HOMAGE
November 1976

The dictator's former aide reports
three hundred thousand killed.
7am, in the dining car serving breakfast, here
morning is open, the season
ripe w/ food.
No tanks in the kitchen.
No one hides in the bush, takes aim, there are
no bullets, just
the random ritual of eggs.
In the dining room innocent passengers
eat their path into the day.
The waiters banter back & forth.
Harry is in the washroom drinking beer.
Alex stands in the pantry, in everyone's road, giving
Information. About his girlfriend.
Three hundred thousand killed.
In the kitchen, the chef careens against fridges,
eyes out of sync, drunk.
Cyclone Todd fries eggs & yells.
His face the same sweaty colour.
Killed.

This moment, this day, to UPI
the dictator's former aide reports
three hundred thousand killed.
In the dining car, now nearly at Wabamun,
sun & bright snow, on schedule, no
bullets, no armed men in the field,
nowhere the obese tyrant shouting *Fire!*
his chest clotted w/ medals, his own people
bloated in rivers, mouths gaped, utter
lost defiance or
the homage no one can know —

GRAN VIA, MADRID

Another room, the voice is singing.
My head full as an unmarked bomb, the music
carries it.
An entire week I lay
in a room above the traffic of Madrid, above
the avenue w/ its scattered proclamations.
& sometimes the voice was a penitent, at the gate
of the cathedral,
sometimes a painted truck, blaring
hymns of the socialista.
Sometimes it was one man alone, fluttering
that rag on a mopstick, & singing.
At last it was just a place, behind
the Cine where someone was stabbed, it spoke the dumb litany
of justice.
How the trafficman stayed in the street's geometry & observed it,
his white gloves gesticulating,
until a truck came w/ police, w/ militia,
to arrest the man
but not the place it happened.

No, the place continues; under seige,
gutted, clattered w/ random bullets; until somehow
a wall remains, & on the wall, just enough room
for a proclamation.
Soon a building is raised, an avenue named, other nations
offer support, more buildings, tungsten is
shipped to a war, now

I lie in a room in the jumbled present,
sick w/ fever in Madrid, like
all you others; saying
it is still your avenue, José Antonio.
It is nobody's dream, & the dream
of all of us, city-dwellers, we
for whom the voice sings in another room, for whom
the lone man dances, & the hymn plays; for us
the penitent stutters at the cathedral gate:
because there is still a place, & a fever,
& room for proclamation; because the voice sings us
ever into the Avenida, gesticulates -
crying words like
La Justicia, No Votar, El Caudillo, El Cristo Rey!

22.05.77/Madrid

9

PHOTOSYNTHESIS

for Karen Shuster

you are old, or are you
young & unsure after all of the climate, the exact
necessity of particulars?
true, certain things can be verified:
you have a job, dental plan, an interest
in vacant houses, probably a motto.
you carry the right grudges, like to say you are
in control, & have no one look up
& state otherwise.
you have a schedule, & adhere to it, at least
in the mornings, if you get up.
after all, the universe has a limited cast
of characters:
& sometimes when you talk in a crowd, you hear
not yourself, but david, how he argued
for years before driving off the highway near lake louise.

how people give you what you never ask for, never want.
how a woman seen today on the street walks
w/ the peculiar gait you had five years ago.
yet then, when you stood in the light
beside the house & had david snap one picture,
& you gave it to me, now it is all i have, it won't answer
my questions, as you did, patiently.
all i can do, is peer, into the picture
& see how the light has changed you, you
are not so tall w/ the house leaning behind,
not so old, or covered w/ vines, yet
your face is white, its smile barely distinguished, your hands
held nervous
together, like a chapel,
one leg slightly behind the other, you stand
bare feet hidden in the lawn, hesitant, smiling
having at last
no words for anything

PULLING THRU
for Paul

Sometimes the invisible pulls
all its blankets away from us.
If only it would stop.
Last night, i saw you on the lake pulling
your brother thru a hole in the ice.
What lake, you say.
From grey water into your arms, the familiar
greeting between brothers, between
good men.
Snow pounded around you, ridiculous
image of white,
skies open like a grey bird, & you moving.
Whole forests of words.
You always wanted to leave like this,
the city & its stalled seasons, leave Main Street
& build a house, somewhere, or in Hope.
Dommage, dommage, but in my dream there were
no houses, only you & your brother & the monstrous
dance of winter, now –

you are singing, your brother
stiff w/ cold, still in your embrace; you are remembering
a whole childhood to him, together,
kissing his shocked head.
Into his ear you feed twenty-year old bread, old doorways,
sour rats, a continent, more & more cabbages!
Finally he nods, mouth twisted open to laugh, his hand
clenched upon yours: he pulls
your arm, rowing it wildly –
he takes you w/ him
across the ice, rowing your faint lives, gladly, like brothers!

RIEL: IN THE SEASON OF HIS BIRTH

1

Riel: *'I hear the voice*
of the wilderness coming
out of the north to meet me.'

prisoner
ponders nicked edge of
photo   grass behind is not
yet knee-high
wavers toward beard   blurred
mouth eroded by spring   poplars
budding sunlit each limb warped
& silent w/ old war
river a flat white
banner against his shoulder   neck
& cheek dissolve in shadow
grey as autumn   Riel
        It is already May –
        You are in the wrong
        season
        Oh where are your armies now

fingers extend thru creased
pockets   palms stiff &
flat against thighs
his wrists revealed

white as broken ice tho spring
will not come to Riel
prisoner of autumn when seasons
became film turned silent
behind his neck
hair fleckt w/ dead

leaves frozen
words lacking sound
as he waits now for white-
lettered FIN to blot final stills   awaits
blank screens   projected flips &
clicks

prairie grass too   halts
in the silent milk of his stare

     2

     Riel: *'I see a gallows*
               on top of that hill, & I
               am swinging from it.'

Riel   the voice flickers
just past your mouth   thick
w/ membrane & unable to
reach you   images lengthen/
distort your opened eyes   Riel
         The grass twists at your
         neck
         Oh where are your armies now

the white horseman fades
fleckt on the painted
screen   alone
against ice-crusted river
& reining toward solitary plains
the troops behind you in confusion
turned to poplars upon hill

       Oh where are your armies now

       Look behind you   Riel
       across water where seasons trespass
       urgent   a child born
in autumn ages gains beard
finds slow cheeks crumpling
to prairie

They are hanging a man
but you are not there
either —
instead stand sloped alone
watch black hangman black
priest in wild craft thru
thick glaze of light

the dead man's head hooked
in chalk-white cap   clad black
coat over shirt   wool nettling
flesh   The embracing is long
            over now   wrists
            pinioned against spine
            moccasins scraping gibbet
            The window unbarred
            prayers finally ended

        Oh where are your armies now

        3

from the dark river
of your brain   the man Scott
stumbles up   canvas-shroud in patches
torn against his cheek   eyes
unbandaged head no longer
bleeding   bullet-wounds white & dry
stains gone from march snow
leaving only the prints of his knees
& fallen shoulder

blood gone also from spring snows
of batoche
of duck lake   leaving only accusations —
words of the priests
spoken against you & the air too thick
w/ sour gods
for reply

14

4

priests & deputies blurred
overexposed   surround gallows
on the poplar hill
surround the man who turns
but cannot warn you   his mustache dark
mouth & eyes eaten too quickly
by shadow

        Why do you watch   Riel
        He is already dead   voices
        knotted in cellulose
        movement/sound
        arrested

        Touch him   Riel
        Reach thru viscous prairie but
        you can't tear this final
        caul   your white fingers leave
        no mark

5

They hang a man & you
are not there   you join
        w/ autumn rivers   ice congealed
        grey at the edge
        your face/beard webbed
        w/ droplets

as trap door jerks down
w/o dangled crack
snapt neck   the man still
leaning fixed in light

        Oh where are your armies now

        Riel   waver thru the death-
        gelled dawn   november returns
        to enfold you now   noosed &   *(no stanza break)*

windless   rivers slowly
w/o energy
poplars frozen on hillside
brittle behind your eyes

while before you   there is this
commotion   your brown-locks clipped
crucifix knocked into dirt   crowds
mumbling in an aftermath
outside the gate   words
you cannot speak nor find
          suspend in thick morning haze
          You gesture madly   twitching
          yet the armies fail
          to recognize you   Riel

          6

Months later   you
regain spring   as march ice
heaves & back-ends   thawing
finally to movement
          & you drop   delivered
hollow in soundless light down
down thru wooden
trap   face still snagged w/
cold leaves
          You plunge deep
          into hillside which does not break
          your falling

          dark body arcs down &
          down   release from the prison
          of autumn birth   & still
          you are falling   Riel

but your voice dangles
wild & liquid   focussed
as grass reborn
          to breathe in the white spring
          of prairie rivers

16

RESPONSIBILITY FOR SHOES

for Aline Kouhi

To find there is a certain
hardness, stored in the heart.
impossible to move around it.
how your silence means it is difficult
to know any word, what can i say then?
too many miles, telephones ringing in empty rooms.
no chance.
or one chance in two years, me holding all
the wrong words, & saying them twice.
you saying nothing, a little, quizzically.

How in the dark you turned
the wrong way down York, coming to visit me:
i stepped from the house & called your name
& you did not hear, just kept walking away;
you, a friend passing thru
just once, looking for me, walking all the miles
back to the Lakehead, borrowed pack on your shoulders,
& me yelling, unable
to move the boulder, the stopped air.
how finally no one notices, or
how what we notice never occurs

Because you did hear, this is history:
you turned & walked up the steps & stayed
four days, left your shoes, returned for them, left again.
how can i be responsible now
for your shoes, for anything else?
did you leave anything here?
i don't want that picture, the one where you keep walking,
the wrong way down York Street.
i don't want to be responsible for that picture.
Wait. Did you leave something?
Stopped like a boulder in my heart.

THIS TIME-WARP IS A DESCRIPTION OF ROBBERS

for Susan Penner

in the hallway, three men mark
walls w/ chalk, at points
where charges will be placed.
They are working to demolish one of the rooms.
To see if the house remains standing,
& what it will say. Surprise
or what. The room is the heart
of the building, has four corners only.
When it is done, ghosts will return
to examine the area
for clean breaks. One w/ pen
will draw them in cipher.
Wait. A woman steps from
the room, declares herself
to be the heart. She knows all the syllables
of detonation. She knows there are other cities
in the universe, but no maps.
She says she has tried to make them.
Her mouth full of chalk & tears...

IT IS MY OWN BONES, CREEPING

Some days it is my own bones creeping
along the wall, insistent as spiders.
My room is a long weaving, at night
its bones tick like a heart, the last one,
abandoned by psychology.
A rumour among the walls says Death
could not be terrible, but my bones
insist on judgement; they want to be judged; it is
their need.
They are sore w/ the argument made
upon their person, who claims, still,
a right to their bad information.
The bones are a loud shouting; they believe
there are infinite particles, but the woman
was never tidy, left them too many hours
on the street w/ no money, no letter of credit, no guarantees.

In their light the bones mark a slow darkness,
ringed w/ nonchalance, ringed w/ fear.
Their marrow speaks softly, in the feudal tongue, words
w/o law because they are a whole family.
A long time in the room, the words embrace one another.
On the wall: the painting of a Saguenay shipyard, one man
has ceased to bear
his arm against the load; now he stands
in the dark corridor slashed w/ steam,
waiting for no-one, holding the hours.

In my country, the politicians talk
of referenda. They do not believe, & while they are not believing
the bones will break loose,
triumphant, singing like birds

✧ from *Wanted Alive*

POST-MODERN LITERATURE

Less to insist upon, fewer
proofs.
Raw metals pulled from the ground, cheaply.
Or a woman in the televised film shouting: thanks to you
I end up surrounded by violence.
So much gratitude, Saturday nights spent
believing in it.

But the end of a city is still
a field, ordinary persons live there, a frame house, & occasionally –
a woman comes out to hang the washing.
From a certain angle you see her
push a line of wet clothes across a suburb.
It sings in the wind there, against
stucco, lilacs, sunken front porches, windows
where nobody moves.
But carefully.   All of it

made carefully, children in snowsuits
after school, appear in the doorway, carry
their tracks shyly.
& you at the kitchen table – your empty
bowl streaked by the spoon, the meal's
memory, papers, juice in one glass, whisky
in another, unwritten greeting cards,
a watch, applesauce, small white medallions.

As if saying the name fixes.
As if the woman will come out again, & pull down
an entire suburb with her washing.
As if the city *could* end, in a field or
anywhere.
or if the woman on the bright TV could
stop saying *thank you*.
or you, saying "like this", & pointing shyly.
Too much paper, the children
in their snowsuits holding doorways, white snow,
parrots singing smuggled information, the corporation gone to

Guatemala.
Leaving Father, the curling rink, a woman dressed
in grey parka & the nearest boots pulling
stiff clothes away from the weather, the back road, post-modern literature

IT IS ONLY ME

for Aline Kouhi Klemencic

Say there is a woman
in the locked-up cornfield.
She is making a desert for herself, not me.
Like the poet said: Fumbling the sky's queer wires,
asking for
mercy, abstract collusion, a kind of awe;
she hikes across the frozen furrows in mid-November
ready to observe almost anything,
self-consciously, as if the turned dirt
would see her singing,
would answer with arguments on Kandinsky & Klee.

At least she can't hear
the saxophone playing scales in the next room,
taking the colours out of the air;
they become discordant sounds & no longer answer.
The words stay silent on the page, their usual selves,
picking lice from under their collars,
not yet torn, or interested, or censored,
or even free.
There are never enough groceries, does the woman
know this in the strange field?
Probably she has thought of it before, a few minutes,
but now the long furrows
are turning her over & over, like a leaf
in the wind.

Never mind the sound,
the saxophonist is in another century, its mountains
stop him from reaching her.
It is only me, with my bad language, my long distance whisky:
I see her far away, it is very cold, I am
calling her out of her field.

KISSES NOT WHISKY

Sometimes there is an emptiness huge
as a bottle of whisky,
hard & glass, caught inside me –
I want to fill it with love of the world,
not whisky.

& not gasoline.
Sometimes it's a Molotov somebody threw there, & it wedged
in my stomach, fizzing, the wet odour
of rags choking me, stuffed into the whisky bottle,

ignited & thrown.
I want to take the hard bomb out, & fill its gap
with kisses, not whisky.

You lean your head on me & my body trembles,
sweating, the clocks tick
with our watches & the sink-drip; & the sound of peaches
outside in the tree.
The dusk is silent as a dead woman come home, afraid to enter.

Even the peach tree was lifted into my life by the stars.
The empty gulp that won't fill, you
get up & drink from the tap,
I can't stop your drinking with my eyes.
I can't eat enough, or the right food, or shut off the clocks –
they uncoil my veins all night like damp hoses,
worn out after so many fire-bombings.

In the body   shock troops have taken cover.
Without whisky the emptiness sticks like a painted door:
I hear the sink drip on the other side, & the peaches rolling,
& a woman tossed in damp bedsheets
unable to reach me, & me
Too frightened to open

BLISS

Bliss on the cats!
Your heaven was suffering for you
until it drowned.
Outside, the cats on the hard fence above the snow, they are
the horizon stepping closer & closr
until distance is just white,
cut-off from us
A horizon of stippled fur moving across the snow, snow
falling even into the ocean,
its grey descent holds us. Without it we are lonely
as a prairie is.
The cook fallen out of the train near Artland,
his white clothes on the track, snow around him,
his body
It could be he was lonely, as an ocean is lonely,
pulling the soft tongues of snow into it,
making its tides alone
Men & their measurements clotted on the shore
Cold surety, dim
beings in their skins, consoling each other.
Bliss on the cats!
They've got away now.
The cook fell not in the ocean but
in Saskatchewan, a horizon pulled him under.
The dream that came explained everything:

Your heaven was suffering for you
until it drowned,   it said.
So bliss on the cats,
pulling the horizon like so much cardboard.
He was alone forever, when the next train came

23

SENTENCES

for Mary Grendys Mouré

1

The short & bumpy sentences of the heart.
Arms of a sweater, bumping
other sweaters in the dark closet.
The crack of air let inside by the dog.
Breathe easy, your mothers
have gone away in cars, dressed in furs, to the sore
hospital of the body.
The heart crouches under the ribs, its beat like a rosary.
Your friends have caved in,
their lips are salty, hard; it's hard when
they raise their tongues to you

Speak up!
Your brothers are shaking their father out of the wet
laundry, unfurling him from bed-sheets in the yard,
divorcing him.
He's your father too!

2

The arms of the sweater are   my arms, waiting
patient for the sideways embrace.
The dog left the door open, I can breathe now.
My mother came back & took off her coat,
& hugged me,
knowing how alone I was   & how I cried
when she went away,
to be emptied by hysterectomy

Hey Mary!
Thanks to you I can kiss the salty
lips of my friends, loving them, stuffing my
sweater into them with its wild arms,
guffawing, rejoining
the bumpy heart-tick, my rosary.
My father writes me his long letters freely now,
we talk together about our own name, Mouré.
Even my brothers stumble up into the doorway, a whole
family yapping & not listening,
as if it mattered, Mother –
Let me tell you I am twins with them, holding our arms &
our years up like sentences, coming alive
however apart our births were!

DIVERGENCES

> *"I am of today & of the has-been; but there is some thing in me*
> *that is of tomorrow & the day-after-tomorrow & of the shall be."*
>
> Zarathustra

I am the youngest in a family of boots & shoes
I am the youngest lifting its burnt flag above my head
into the ocean,
recoiling a bit at the cold kiss of water
I am part of a long family lifting its boots out of the mud.
The family sighs in front of me, I watch the backs of
a thousand children growing gaunter, beckoning me.
I follow them for years & years, forever
arriving.

I am the youngest child of a family that cries itself to sleep,
all over the world
Its body unconscious in Argentina after questioning,
shot in Zimbabwe with the shout of joy caught in its mouth,
arrested in Lisbon for *insulting the President*,
gassed in an Afghani hill-town.

Also I am the youngest of a long line of gunners, of proud
trigger-pullers, maintainers of public order,
of supporters of the safety of the state, of the increase
in production: I am the youngest dressed in
white   carrying the Host in cathedrals, singing the glorious
anthem,
singing birth & resurrection for *those who are*
with us

Friend, are you with us? Do you love your
patron with his feudal beneficence, with his
godly benediction, with his new clothes, his whisky & wine,
his descent into the dead

where he found you? Robber, he robbed you.
He took you out of the dead   into the world where you are now,
stumbling with your ancestors, your predecessors, kissing the
lovers who left you after one night, the passengers of trains –
who walk in front of you in their boots & shoes,
a family.

Family of which you are the youngest, barely born, carrying
the same old flag into the sea.
Your eyes pressed open, a light fills them credulously,
the ocean laps at the dryness in your bones.
Is it true you can't go back now?
Go on, says the flag, its burnt edges singing
at the touch of cold water.
Yes, say the family, *yes*, say the boots & shoes,

Go back, cry the gun-shot wounds, opening –

26

SANCTUS

in the hall, the same
lightbulb burnt-out for days, marked
like a beacon.   in spite of.
your face with its torn eyelids
spun by the window, fated charm.

i stand in the chasm between night
& the hours, muscles tight before me, like
the fear i had once, & went bowed
to the lucky priests for forgiveness.
disorderly.   needing a coat.
speak: sanctus, sanctus.

in those days disorder
an offense against government.   the army marched
from my language into yours, wielding
their cherished badges.
hold it, i love you.

holy orders, holy war.
citizens taken without charge: mute, raging.
the same light burnt-out for weeks; too many sudden
corridors.
hard to speak anything, blasphemous words.

in the chasm, cupboard doors crash shut with no favour.
i'm hungry, but i've already eaten
my fingers.
today surgeons touched the pulse in my foot, & jerkt
back, astonished.
when they opened the speculum, my cervix
clenched.

now i can't tell the truth about events or anything.
there are too many orders banging doors.
too many priests, governments, obeisant armies.
hold it, i want
to sing to you.   in spite of.
get out the chasm & wear it, like a ripped coat,
if they arrest you, i'll kill them

BARRINGTON
for Tony Klemencic

There was the hard day you told us of,
nineteen stories into the sky; with your grey
shirt-sleeves rolled, the metal box filled
with tools, hammers,
fixing some thing on the roof of the building.
You couldn't tell us what.
Or if it was sunny.
If it was the shingles, or something to do with the drains.

You told us you worked with an old man, that between
his hands & the tools there was
no withholding.
All day you tried to work as he did, moving slowly
across the roof like a cat
high up into the daylight.
For you this happened;
for us it is just an image like a film, you & this man
nineteen floors up the building on Barrington,
the light is hard, all your arms move together,
tacking the roof, feet spread over it,

you & the workman high above us in the sky.

Then you told us what you dreamed then,
that the roof was done, you both
had turned your arms back thru the sleeves of your jackets,
& locked the tools, when
the old man jumped off the side of the building.
Holding his box of tools, that evening.

& we see you as you tell it, awake with our glasses of beer
on the twelfth floor of the same building, where you live,
gazing with you
into the dark where the old man fell.
How he fell, you told us: like a lamp, like a skiff of paper,
easily, you dreamed him falling like a seed,
slowly, ready to land.
Waiting for you.
& you jumped after him, you too with your tools.

It was like jumping off a stair, you said, when you landed.
You had seen the whole city thru its haze, the sun
pushing the lake into the towers, the light
as it sparked
each window in your long floating,
nineteen stories to the street & the old man outside the door.

Then we take our beer again, the same grainy film
of your dream runs past us, its defiance of the layered city,
the people in their houses along Barrington
eating dinner,
& your jacket floating, sunset, the hard speck that was
the box of tools, & your wild trust of the man,
that carried you down to us

from *SEVEN RAIL POEMS*

1

Fraser Canyon

for the waiters & waitresses

The train wrests
the sun out of the rocks,
buckled rocks that make the light grow
huge on the mountain-side
Trees & transmission lines blazing long wires thru the scars
Above them –
Clouds, fierce & silent
torn across the buttresses & edged darkly
Saw-tooth trees glancing thru their huddled argument
Their song without name
or recognition
Power carried down from the dams
to cities by the sea

Wheels sing against the rail, shearing metal, the train pulls
mightily
snaking down the Canyon with us
caved in its belly
as our hunger grows us weary, weary
Workers awake half the night
in the closed kitchens drinking beer
Sliding arms across each other
Lovers of humans, of steel   diesel trains, of the long
race across the Valley
Lovers of kisses
Servers of food

2

VIA: Tourism

Always, the same bodies
slumped in rows, the same questions & fear
of accident or delay
The words of technique, comfort
dealt out to strangers in the wheels' rough noise
The jagged train of hours

Then there are the women   beaten by their husbands
who bear the marks as they bore their children,
without disgrace,
who bring their children away with them
across the country in coach seats or
jammed into one berth
drinking pepsi, eating aspirin
Locked in the motion of rails, of constant arrival
Their bruised eyes & hands swollen
from battering tables
Insistent
Children tangled among their legs
Vacant of husbands
Wondering, alone
Gone where they've never been, moving into their lives
with no more father

Above all this, for miles & days, the habitual
tourism that never stops, the PR rep in her blue coat
saying VIA, VIA

We Are A Trade

Sometimes people clutter in aisleways, holding
unspent money,
their eyes tired, by days travelled
in broken airconditioning,
the sun & prairies cut in their bodies, their stance –
You can't say you don't see
Pythagoras,
the immigrant Canadian sending money home;
he's out there in his lousy field of rapeseed
on New Holland equipment, cutting
one yellow swath from the horizon.
Some will call this impossible
politics.
Pythagoras will turn his tractor toward the train.
His belief bends the earth & grows.
Wheat corporations take the money, America –

In the train, passengers eat & return
to watch & drink whisky,
speak old aphorism –
the duck-lakes of Saskatchewan, money in Alberta,
Valley farmers dead in their silage
& us, employees, members
of the union who won't vote anymore
who serve doggedly
18 hours every day, who work dogged
For the time off at home, whole afternoons spent
in poolrooms, or sleeping
Affluent in dreams, paying rent in public housing

What do you expect from me
We earn dividends for no one
We watch Pythagoras & prime ministers from the same train
flat & curious
We are a stubborn trade

♦ **from** *Domestic Fuel*

LUNGE

All of a sudden you find out there isn't enough time.
You find out there was never enough time.
You find out you shouldn't have washed the dishes.

Over & over, so many dishes, the wet cloth, the spill
across the counter, window, bird out there
or not, the clean house, begin

& you find out you shouldn't have bought the clocks.
You shouldn't have bothered buying clocks.
You never had what they had to measure.

You leap up & throw them face-down into the trash.

There is not enough time to cry about this.
The pain in your back is very deep
& pointless.
You find out that all this time they said
you were part of the working class
there was no time.
The real working class in this country was always unemployed,
& you always had a job, the same one.

You find out there is no such thing as enough time
& still you don't have any of it.
You shouldn't have craved the arms of women.
You shouldn't have slept with men.
You shouldn't have dreamed *Philosophy*, or
the heart monitor screen in your apartment bedroom,
just like in emergency.
It's all shit. Merde. This, & hey, & you others.

33

Time for the medicine. You fast cure. You fuck-up mad dog. You you. You lunge over the table. In mid-lunge. Going for the adrenalin again, going for keeps, prose, boots, the sandwich you couldn't eat, you bit & spit out, you thought it would make you sick again. Lunge for the dog's stale portion of sleep, your legs straight off the chair, your hair stuck out, the clatter of the chair falling backward, zone five, zone six, the sound of

Your arms make

Amicus, object,   referent

Points   of or-   der

IDIOM BIRDS

The cars in the shut lot are burning their doors.
Sandwiches unravel their tongues,
sucking the mouth.
All the idioms have been written out.
Modernity is a hard beak, to cherish.
Unwrite idiom.
Tip over idiom, tailless haunted bird,
stable currency,
that which speaks,
that which wanders, cloud with trousers,
yo-yo,
brink, my sad revolver, my door.

Open up or be stolen, passing sentence
in the getaway car,
gunning its verbs like a motor.
Unseal.
Unrip & sew, bluster, speak, who listens, who hears
or writes
unless I'm smirking, pulling phrase
out of the cupboards, idiom birds
Come on, birds
trying to dance their bone skulls
on the window
hard syllables named Apollinaire, their guns
thrown in the gas tank,
trapped birds,
my idiom, soft idiom, tastes like hay

LIKE THEATRE

A woman describes her
life as the decreasing width
of beds
King-size bed, double bed, & now single bed
Measures the air with her hands
Hot air
Islands of air
When the morning comes what does it matter
the woman ends, laughing,

& directs the music in the restaurant for her friends

Upside-down music, she says
like theatre

SHOCK TROOP

Shock troop
shock exercise
Knife is a verb
Bayonet a verb
Coat a verb
Absolute is a conjunction
Now get up & pay for the coffee,
make a sentence, fool

She knife, she coat, absolute she bayonet
he said
incomprehensible as
shock troops blowing the door in
& taking the TV down stairs to a truck

You don't pay me, you live here
she said, pushing his money back, the tip, too

SPIRIT-CATCHER

What I am is never clear, is the heart
lonely, is a word, dusk,
bed-eaten
Love, I am the veined-blue iris in your hand
when you clench fists
breaking over nothing
I'm the dust during years of renovation, the pulse
of cats
The disturbance of light, the still loaf of rye
The shudder, ecstasy you bring me
as if it were grace, or usual

My body is the thing you see that's slowly
dying,
the first clock of the phone
before a ringing
It won't focus cleanly in the hemisphere we're in

where women are hungry & the dead are pushed full of bread
& sewn
An excess in the mouths of presidents
who talk of the nation's *sanctity*, the right to *pray*
of which there is none
We pray without right, as we must

just as I drink, to get out of my body,
out of the light's psychic noise on my skin
It's said the spirit leaves us thru the mouth, which
is why I speak to you
The maps of my body fail me, a sheer bulk
stopping transmission
closing shop
My silence, deaf as radar

WHAT THE WOMAN REMEMBERS OF HER DYING, ON THE STREET BEFORE THE AMBULANCE CAME

The core that eludes me, the words
un-spoken,   pulled back into the tongue.
It is the tear-space inside the wall, where
the seventy years are waiting,
their mouths round with o's.
It is the seven nights of the body.
The beginning of the spine.
Sleep without measure.
Sash flung up & down.
Outside in.
It is the air.
When it meets my face, my mouth opens.
It is not fear.
It is what we fear.
It is the green trees rushing upward from the boulevard.
It is green everywhere.
It is not the hung figure.
It is not maleness.
It is grass. It is the tree.
It is the sound of hands.

INCLUDING MYSELF

Everybody who has lived in Vancouver, ever.
Everybody who has lived in Vancouver
for ten years.
Everybody who has had a job, a jacket, drink
when they need it, at a price
they can afford.
In ten years there is no molecule in the body
that is the same.
What identity is, has been overworked
in these pages.

The small snow under the birch near Morley
Alberta.
How this is a trick to say
small snow.   *(no stanza break)*

37

My brother fumbling with his camera & frowning,
checked shirt & muddy boots,
standing in the highway ditch under the birches,
black cloud over him.

In ten years my brother came to see me in Vancouver
three times.
On the average, once every three years,
with one year over.
We pounded our feet on the floor
singing London Homesick Blues till the woman
from downstairs came up to remind us
her husband was dying of cancer
& did not want to hear our feet or
London Homesick Blues.
Whatever.

None of the molecules are the same in their bodies either.

My brother is in Toronto on the top floor of
a house, going to school.
When he was in Morley, he was a groundskeeper.
Now just out his kitchen window is a small
tin screaming-porch.
Who knows who started this name but this is
what it is called.
It leads nowhere. You can only scream from it.

Everybody who has lived in a Canadian city, including
myself.
In ten years none of the molecules of our bodies
will be the same as now.
We should get to know each other
quickly.
We should rejoice.
We should walk into the street or onto the screaming-porches,
before we are too
different or too changed,
& call out, offering each other
our future absence, our private & immoderate discourse,
the place where we are hoarding
memory, & the small snow

FENTIMAN AVENUE

The roses are out along Fentiman Avenue.
I get up out of my chair & ask
my father if there were roses.
I cross out the line.
The roses are out in the gardens along Fentiman Avenue.
I am out looking for the three Billys.
One of them grew up to be
my Dad, but I am not looking for my father.
The roses are out in the soft dirt of Fentiman Avenue.
The three Billys are in their ripped t-shirts
in the shade, if possible.
The houses are full of dust & cat hair, &
the dogs are ornery.
There was Billy Mouré, Billy Hall, & Billy Maubach.
The roses are out along Fentiman Avenue.
I am not sure if there were
ever roses.
I was eight years old when my father showed me
the house on Fentiman for the first
& last time.
I get up out of the chair & go to the window.
My father is walking up & down Fentiman Avenue.
I know this is true.
He is one of the three Billys.
It happens to be August.
In the picture there are roses.
I cross out the line.

LIONS

It's all new.
We are angels splitting theological hairs
or party jokes, or just
a piece of cake with jam in the middle,
the way my mother made it for our birthdays,
Ken's birthday when he got the hamster,
that died after biting Steve Tzeckov.
We could see Steve's garage from our house, & his new fence.
From our kitchen window where the light came
thru green ruffled curtains
my mother sewed after the night classes.
Under the kitchen table where I lay while my father
kicked out at me, yelling
Get up! No one is hurting you!
Later, Steve Tzeckov died of cancer.
He never did drink anything at the neighbourhood
Christmas parties.
That's the kind of man a family wants, my mother said.
We listened gravely, drinking up the rum
in our root beer & fighting each other
in the basement.
That was later.
We felt sorry for the rest of the Tzeckovs.
Or I felt sorry.

When I think of it, I can still see his garage.
Between it & his house, a small space
where you could see the park paid by the Altadore Lions.
I saw my brother out there once, the day the dog
got run over by a bread truck.
Between the houses, he was so small, screaming.
You could hear him in our kitchen over a block away.
That's the kind of man a family wants, my mother said.
He finished the new fence before he died.
How do they get enough to eat, I wondered.
There's some kind of pension, she said.
My brother was outside screaming.
Steve was one of the Lions.
The space between the houses was so small.

40

CHERISH

for Libby Scheier

The expression of longing,
in & among
the collapse of social systems,
among facts such as fish see colour;
in a room where light cannot enter the high window,
where mugs are empty of coffee & contain
so many ounces of the room's air,

in the room where air dips close
between the arms,
where women are not forgetful any longer
but tell their whole stories
& fear their body's message,
being alone

The essential barrier
The unknown way to cherish aloneness
& dispel it as a waste
The cups are empty on the floor all night long,
the plates have tipped their crumbs into the paper,
the paper has lain stubbornly unread
until its news is no more sensible,

until Salvador is liberated or invaded,
the fish are suffocating in their own waters,
the future has occurred & not been announced yet
Women
in the ease of their voices' murmur,
able to express but not dispel
anything
To talk without loneliness
because it has been acknowledged & achieved
in our own bodies
Because here the cups are full of the noise
of our laughter,
because no touch is the answer & we know it giddily
& The longing for it
purely
makes us full

SOME OF THE WOMEN

Some of the women I know look like the men I imagine.
Some of the woman I know are
wearing blue silk softly this year.
Some of the men I know look like, crazily, & look away.

At the side door, the man with light shirt
& upturned collar leans forward,
holding his hand out from his body,
he points it toward the door jamb & turns

He lifts one arm, no one is watching, before he enters
he touches the future, like silver, like a blade,
a small cut in the sky close to his fingers,
like computer satellite

Some of the women I know are wearing dresses
with prints of sailing boats on blue
& pants underneath that.
Some of the women I know are dancing, I know

they are still dancing, the light flashed
on their front & sides makes their bodies
jump jaggedly in the air,
never touching the dance floor

ever again.
I want the men I know to look like women.
I want the men I know to stop imitating us & be someone.
I want the men I know to stop inventing.

As if you can lie about your dreams

GILLS

The seven kinds of pain of which we are speaking.
The small bones of the fish peeled up
& outward from the eaten body,
a cage on which our sight is fixed,
seeing the fish
jump out of the light blue chop
of water.
Alone, the pain is, pulling
the bent hook out of the fish's lip,
the fish struggling its smooth muscle.
Or the girl who waded up to her boot tops
in an icy current, shooting the fish
with a .22, or just
kicking it upward, out of the water.

The pain from which we speak, we speak
to pull the hook
of our words thru the other's lip, nearest the bone,
tearing it, saving the hook.
I remember Dogpound Creek on the neighbour's
property, fishing with my brother for the speckled browns,
my cast leapt back up the wet bank
& caught his eye.
How he cried out & I was afraid before I saw him,
wanting to change what I knew had happened,
wanting the cry to be a bird.
In some dreams the fish are tinsel in the trees,
the fish are cardboard painted brightly,
the fish smell bad when they fry
if they come from the sewer pipe, where they'd rest sometimes.
It softened their flesh,
when fresh caught
they were already rotten, you could put your hand
into their fishy sides.

We believed this.
In the dark, feeling our hands on the ice flow,
climbing the cliff away from the river,
our pants crusted with cold, hard,
the sound of the ice breaking in the darkness below.
Restless pain of which I am speaking.
In the mornings, I am drugged with salt & cold.
Some of the fish have scales that must be removed before eating
Some of the fish are rising with their teeth in black rows.
My hands grip into the softness of their gills.
My fingers are wet & the gills lift open, involuntary.
It is what the pain allows.
It is the start of food.

BLINDNESS

Some of our desires are known only on the floor
of oceans, the nets dragged thru,
a light beyond colour we can't imagine, where we live now,
people of the surface,
whose foetuses still bear gills for a few days
& lose them, our kinship,
the water inside women,
water where we form & grow.

The halibut frozen whole, a sheet of memory,
held up, thawed, cut into slices
across the body, the central location of the spine,
our shared spine,
small bone hands of its vertebrae,
evolved away from us.

To feed us, first & lastly, taste
of white flakes upon the tongue,
soft resistance to the teeth & jaw;
our body is water &
the fish burn in it like fuel.

The flatfish that begins like any other,
swims upright
buoyant in the water, one eye on each side
of the head.
Then adolescent, feeling the body stagger
& list, gone sideways, one eye
migrates across the forehead or
thru the skull
to the right or left side, depending on the species.

Some of our desires are known only here,
are only now being let loose & admitted,
have only this moment stopped being
ashamed,
ashamed of the shape our bodies took & stayed on land
when the fish said No & went back
into the water,
mistake, mistake, fuck the lungs, some of our desires
are known only on the ocean floor, in the head

of the flatfish, halibut lying on its left side,
the eye that migrated across its skull
staring upward with the other.
At rest with it, patient.
Some of us have lungs that suffocate in the air.
The human body, two eyes fixed in the skull,
a third eye that presses on the forehead
& gets nowhere, presses & lives,
its silence the silence under oceans,
in the deep water of the body,
its blind side facing the brain

GOODBYE TO BEEF [2]

The irrational deafness of our heads, that's
all.
Where our elegant coiffure comes from,
our own fingers, hey: squirrel-
hunting in the Rocky Mountains under the smell of spruce
forest I said I never would forget
& haven't.
Damn it.
Where our research will get us,
home free, sliding fast
past the hard throw from second baseman.
Looking for just one more homer.

We are listening to too much music, & our tastes
are lousy.

The squirrel my brother shot down with the .22 so the dog could play.
The dog just sniffed the dead fur
& looked up the tree again, eye
cocked for the squirrel.
It is always in our damn heads.

Or my head.

Or anyone's.

When we got together, what we talked of,
the moose my uncle shot & cut up into frozen pieces,
& sent it down, in 1964, on the Greyhound.

What I forgot to say, was:
When we saw that box of moose hefted out of the bus bay in
the din of yelling navvies,
we knew it was goodbye to beef
till springtime.

& I haven't talked to my aunt since.

I go deaf thinking of it. Or anything.

PURE REASON: HAVING[3]

Having the most to lose.
Having a steadie gaze, &
most of all, a haircut.
Having sent everything to the laundry, even
the unlaunderable.
Having a *photocopy* of a page of *writing* taken
from a *magazine*.
I am in the car of my father with a mug of sweet coffee
outside Red Deer Alberta in the white of winter
wearing the coat I've had twelve years
& not liking the coffee, either.
Between Edmonton & Calgary, the roads are closed by snow.
Drifts on the highway & hard wind
moving who knows where.

Having forgotten my destination
Having been capable of shyness
Having been shy
Having kissed my family on their nearest shoulders

What the highway is, pointing without slope or vision.
Its re-constructed dream
empty, finally
except for the curves & overpasses, the centre median.
To be, always, capable.
To move the jaw in & out, as if biting
hard.
To be reckless.

To be on the road. This early.
Wherever we are going.
Wherever my parents drive.

Seated ahead of me. Their heads faced away.
Sculptures of apples.
The cold visible, white

PURE REASON: SCIENCE[4]

The day the animals came on the radio, fed- up, the electrodes in their hands
beaming, small tubes leading into their brains where chemicals enter,
& the bubbling light from that, the experiment
of science,
the washed fur on their faces & in their voice

The quick brown fox jumped over the lazy dog is a comparison we reject,
they say. Leading to the obvious:

Maple _sugar_ comes from maple _trees_.

Animals in the laboratories, their small chests
cut open where the wires are, the tough protective hairs & sensory
reception, high-pitched hearing,
on the radio, sonant, re/
plying to science that is hurting them for diet soft drinks,
they say,
how the light of our poisoned colons shines
its fine beam into the cells of animal brains
As if you could dream like we dream & be cured, the animals say,
pushing back the announcer,
showing off into the microphone the cut scars
of our diet fantasy
inside which their babies are waiting with our defects
to be born

PURE REASON: FEMININITY

The day the women came on the radio, fed-up, electrodes in their purses
beaming, small tubes leading into their brains where doctors enter,
the bubbling light from that, neuronic balance, the de/pression
of their inner houses,

washed skin on their faces & in their voice

She belongs to a certain class of women whose
profession is to promote lust is a comparison we reject,
they say to the judge. Leading to the
obvious:

Deathful *thinking* comes from deathful *minds*.

Women in the earth are not so powerless, their soft chests
torn open where the pin-ups were, the tough protective skin & sensory
reception, the high-pitched hearing,
on the radio, their subjective loudness, sonant, re/
plying to justice that divides them into classes,
they say,
how the light of the soft cock under the black robe shines
its fine beam into the cells of women's brains
As if you could dream like we dream & be cured, the women say on the
radio,
pushing back the announcer,
showing off into the microphone the cut scars
of obstetrics out of which their babies have been pulled out, held
by doctors, newly *born*

OCEAN POEM

I am the one who lies, slowly, closer
to your arm.
I insinuate.
The trip trip of the rain into wet earth &
the traffic noise.
This kind of a hush[1], she said.
Lifting her arms over her head so gently
in a gesture of, longing.
We are all innocent beings with our bathtubs[2] & literary
pure enforcement.
I don't know if there's any difference between men & women[3]
is just a lie.[4]
The word human being has stood for men
until now.

Until now.

When she puts her arm down, in innocence,[5]
I'll show her.[6]

---

[1]*There's a kind of a hush, all over the world, tonight*
All over the world, you can hear the sound of lovers in love.
                                                    Herman's Hermits, 1966

[2]Places to get clean. Large, enamel, clumsy. "Bathtub gin."

[3]The poets who say this believe that the standard of poetic
  excellence is just excellent & not male.

[4]This should not be done in any poem, accusing someone of lying.

[5]In no sense.

[6]Read "shore". This is an ocean poem.

VILLENEUVE[12]

He held up his hands so we could see the handcuffs.
He stepped off the plane & held up the handcuffs so we could see his hands.
Out of the small white-painted plane he stepped & raised his arms so we could see the handcuffs on his hands.
Out of the small plane rivetted carefully by union labour & painted white
he raised his hands with the cuffs on them.
So we could see his hands locked together with the handcuffs he stepped out of the plane holding his arms upward.
When the plane landed, three RCMP entered & emerged with him in handcuffs.

On the tarmac he was escorted by the RCMP.
On the tarmac after stepping out of the small plane painted white with his arms in the air so we could see the handcuffs he was escorted by the RCMP.
When the plane landed, the RCMP entered it & emerged with him.
Before he stepped into the car he waved his hands so we could see.

BETTY[16]

O darkness & the empty moons, women
speaking light words into the cups of each other's fingers.
Or the mouth that fills a whole room, whispering
black air, not saliva, & not im/
pertinence.
We are here forever, unspoken, our undershirts stick in the room's heat,
stick between the breasts, in the flat place over the bone
that holds the chest
from tearing open, like the metal traps' cold tensity
where we laid them rusted in the city river,
drown-set for muskrat
Our small hands frozen, without fingers, claws of ice holding stiff snouts of fur,
strange sprung words leaking

into our sentences.
"A-girls ", the 2 year old girl called out at the supper table.
Let's not say "Grace" again, she said, let's say "Betty".
In the second public grade of school there were
5 Johns & 3 Debbies, 3 Darlenes, 2 Tims,
most of them grew up called Didi or Evan, & I stared out the window
at the racks of bicycles, tipped any way over, flat prairie line-scape,
the one consistent image I have of school.

Why are so many women lonely, empty as the inside of bicycles, as
the mouths using all the room,
the boys in their tight jeans &
slimness that will leave them in their 22nd year,
the boys & their hard laugh who is tougher,
boys getting at each other's love, thru the inside
of women, their intermediary, their confessional.

I want to speak sexually of one thing – not male love
but physical knowing: the distance
between the breastbone & the palm, the two
important parts of the body.
Where the water runs in the long veins, curving thru space.
The palm where you can dive in & drink & never come up again,
& forgive no one, & feel, as you break the surface –
your head wet, streaming, smelling faintly of milk or oranges

from *The Acts*

— 6 —

Then if the surface haunts me. If there is a name <u>surface</u> then what else is there. Is what is "different" from the surface <u>depth</u> or is it <u>another surface</u>. The language imposes dualism on our thought. Which must be broken, so to, speak. *How when the line is written there is blank page below, into which the signs are moving.*

Can I, in writing the next line, refuse what haunts me on the surface of the page, with its easy affirmation. *Be lyric. In my image. In my image. Forty lifetimes in the desert with the mouth pushed shut...*

The emotional "depth" under the surface is NOT the culture that occupies the page, inherited from the visible only. It is behind that. Either we pass behind or are we excellent beings.

Or sexual. If our "depth" is choked at the surface, becomes a sexual problem. Lady MacB. saying ye gods unsex me now. Where our female sex is without consequence we must cast it off to act, to speak. Or wear the cast the culture offers us: the surface of the page.

The blind calf with the membrane over its head, tottering in the darkness, the wall of the house near it, it feels the warmth of indoor heating. The membrane choking in its mouth, should it choose to eat it? Its mother still labours, giving birth to its twin. Smaller, lighter, shrivelled. If the blind calf lives it is because it learned inside its mother to take that space from its own twin. Inside the womb. Where it was so dark, does it ever need vision again?

What is key to this desire: To have one's existence affirmed by others. Or, put oneself at risk forever (a panic at the cell's edge). Or is it affirmation, first, that then makes the risk possible? To bear it. The risk of, kissing her.

The embrace first, then the utterance.

What this need for affirmation meant before, was having an existence affirmed by men. Knowing how they praise well what affirms their relation. They do not have to put them-selves at risk, which women have always had to do, to exist, to speak, to have their existence affirmed by others.

What I had not spoken! The way she cried out because of my silence, & how I chose it, stubborn. My defense of necessity. Because my eyes and my whole body could see that the words and bodies of women were not listened to or affirmed.

But we women listen so carefully to each other. The resurrection of the woman's body is of Kore, not the phallic king-dom. This affirmation is the true necessity. To inhabit freely the civic house of memory I am kept out of.

Oh!

To take the movement of the eye that is <u>seeing</u>, and use it to make the reading surface of the poem.

On the radio, the arrival of the exiled terrorist who is an ordinary human who was so angry twenty years ago, how the description highlights the raised arms and handcuffs, you hear it on the morning news every 10 minutes, those two physical details. Because they are, in the end, what is important; there is no "event" apart from the handcuffs. In a painting this is where there would be the most light, right where the handcuffs are. If not light, then darkness. Or a skull and an open book, a tree, a leaf. Or ciphers from tombs, iconic. *Guil Apol.*

And the eye would transmit this light message to the brain over and over. As if we are looking at a painting; as if the eye is looking for the first time, curious, at a painting or photograph, the rapid movement of its gaze transmits the surface to us, until either the real becomes abstracted, or the abstraction of light on the page becomes real. And the handcuffs themselves are marks of punctuation, bearing the two dark commas of the hands.

The poem is not called "Terrorist" because "terrorist" is a word conferred by those who have already taken power. The poem is about the exile, who is not what is terrible. It is the co-incidence of the police like an embrace. And the bracelets.

—— 14 *(excerpt)* ——

***

What I brought back to poetry from my job was a stutter that
replicated surfaces imperfectly, like the television screen with the
vertical hold broken, no story possible, just the voices

heard again & again without image. Those dark voices. & I wrote,
not into the book's heart, but out of fear, to make the image come
back to me. Any image. My coat & shoes. My faint moving at the
edge of the screen, blood in my head not moving but the room
moving & the blood still... so that to move the force <u>for a moment</u>
only <u>held</u> for that moment. (The word "held" a stillness, relational,
not a motion...) (The word "moment" not a thing...) The preposi-
tion so relational it could not hold a <u>value</u>, & could hardly keep from
vanishing.

I still believe in the relations & not the name. The symbol of relation.
Hidden tensity of the verbs without tense. Because the past tense
exists IN us speaking, or is not anywhere. We can speak of it
separately because our language permits it. The future tense too.
They do not exist outside our bodies! But in us as memory, & desire.
Those <u>relations</u>.

& If we are to free our memories, our desires, we must refuse to
<u>restrain ourselves</u>

✧ **from** *WSW (West South West)*

THE JEWEL

The light air struck her, going in, the doorway
& its silver paper,
so festive

The light air struck her past the room's whirl & elevator
What was in her head, then,
likely

or not failed her, failed her here at last, in the office

The light room just an office
with its stained chair & terminal & fluorescent tube
the cup with its rhyme no

rime of coffee out of the brown machine where the red
light stares all day saying ononon ononon ononon
& nonono

So she dyed her hair red
So she dyed her hair red again when it faded
So she wore a red jacket
So she listened for the sound of her monthly blood
So she listened to her hair
So she listened to the soft fold of her jacket

The light over the desk, what can she do?
The phone speaking out of its cradle, what can she do?
The chair shaped physically for beauty, dulling her back, what can she do?
The green light notation of the screen, what can she do?

There are days we feel we are repeating, from some other time, we get
out of bed with the fish taste wet gills capsized boat of sleep
in our mouths & eyes rubbing as if the day has punctured
our careful wall, wall of dream, wall of physical memory
where the body knows itself, not gratuitous
Oh memory said Vasyl Stus, the sound of the Dnipro/
not gratuitous the dream punctured by the sound of alarm
& the hard faces of the wall, the wall, the other wall, four
walls of the room

These days I dream of the wet dawn smell of willows & the fishing rod
held high over the head, over ground cover, not
to be entangled,
the red & white jewel at the end of my line, dreaming its metal dream of
water, & me in the jacket too small
for the sweater I am wearing &
just this,
not being young or too young but being my age,
the age I am,
the wet dawn smell of the willows

My tongue like salt, not made for speaking
My tongue the colour of ice, what ice thinks before the storm
its crust clear in the dip of pavement
My eyes with their fine wrinkles, my eyes the eyes of my mother,
my tongue a bit of her knitting, where it came from,
her womb

I think of my father who went for years each morning to the office.
In his car.
Cutting the ice off the car's windows with a plastic handle.
Wearing a wool scarf.
Wearing a wool coat & handcuffs underneath that.
Wearing a belt, suspenders, glue, mahogany trimming, nails & screws, a shirt
with a package of cigarettes over the heart, a story of the air force, *the time that,
there was the time that, sometimes, in that time, in those times*

Even, I think, in prison, far from
the town one knows, far from that territory & its river; in *Perm* in Russia, in
Kingston on the side of the lake, cold, invisible passage beyond the wall,
the white ice & mouths of the carp,
their eyes sensing light & darkness,
it doesn't matter whose prison,
I think, one uses, for memory, the present tense

We are fishing in the cold river, emblem of the stream of blood leading
in & out of the heart, its loveliness manifest, the dawn
on the river, shallow, where the fish can't hide, where
in fact no one has caught fish,
who search the lonely pools of darkness & stay away from the dawn light
It hurts them
Dawn light
Red

The thyme in the mouth risen gorging the head full of sleep, I
wake up, am waking, my body alone naked house silent
around the wall, bed, drug of sleep, oh my drug
my hands warm tongue soft sheet in the mouth taste of thyme & silver
frost, on the window, light enters, the jewel light enters &
the darkness, begins

So she dyes her hair red
She wears her hair red
She wears the red coat of her blood
Soft tenderness
Soft smell of the thyme

What I miss is the absence of the image & tie to landscape, I, who am
hugely tied to the smell of yellow grasses & the sage, I, who am attracted
to the dry hills of the Peloponnesus, I walk out in them & press their
smell to my face & they smell crazily like the hills of Cochrane Alberta,
my heart lives in that dry corona & smell of sage

So her hair is red
So her hair is still red
So she runs her fingers dreaming thru her red hair
So her hair shudders
So she shudders
Her small, heart shudders
Her hand is red

My genitals covered, soft surface of the water red dawn light
the rod carried wall of sleep head of sleep corn porridge flat in the belly
flat cloth above genitals my genitals, my folded labia neat envelope &
warm put away fishing,
put away the green coat its memory of the pools where the rubber boots
lie, & tipped grocery carts, & grey slime from
the storm drains, street overflowed

put away your genitals
Gently

I am trying to think of the seven uses of the past tense.
Self-hatred, self-pity, guilt, fear of the body, separation from the mother,
trials in public court,

The office. I have to go to the office. Where I work. Today I have to get up
& go to the office. I have to comb my hair. I have to look like. I have to
speak without laughing. I have to wear my sweater. My hair. My hair
arrayed how how how. My light heart trips me & the darkness begins. I
am not malevolent. What will I do with my writing. I want to fail to
understand notation. & the sounds. Aphasia. I love you. My readers, I
will be able to kiss you. The dryness of my lips. I warn you. What we
are given to understand. What we are given. Begs the question. One
question. So I can kiss you. The words kiss & question unconnected
until now

from *THE RAINSHORE: FIELD, RAIN, HEAT*

FIELD

My soul is out of the hospital.
Puts its grey leaves into the sun,
as if, special.
Or just shy. The grey
of it
stings some,
stings, some.

The soul with the narrow structure of the line,
post, lintel, post.
The way we say: doorway,
so the soul can open
& walk thru,
holding a glass
of water.

The way a doe walks,
becomes still
when its ears
shift.

The field opens. My brother
bends down, cuts open
the deer's stomach.
Part of the field is here.
We are breathing.

The light is that light
before the storm comes,
my brother won't look up
now. The storm
will ruin him.

We are all these
souls. The lines
are thin here.

FIELD 2

A field without birds doesn't
make sense, she said, the
more birds the better, they
eat there, gorge on the loose grain.
Their soft blue oil, feathered.
Their noise

kisses the blood
It is this kiss
keeps us

out of, the hospital

FIELD 3

Two damp children turn
on the beds, outside
the hospital is
the river, boys with
ice cream, a few shouts
& the willows wherein
sweet brown flickers
make their crazy
crazy
noise

All words are said with the most beautiful accent.
The children have sore
throats, are excised
of one thing:
tonsils.

FIELD 4

I wish she would just stick to the stomach of the deer.
Inside the deer, we find
everything we need for
the next stage:

lungs, a liver, kidneys, colon, the heart.

The deer lies on the ground, its legs out.
The television of its eyes sees
my brother with the knife, from
about x many degrees of daylight,

its skin lying open, listening
to us talk about the fixed price
of grain, this year,
the storm above

FIELD 5

We will now return to the hospital the soul came
out of. With no tonsils. & never went back in.
Just heard the nurse's stories, who came in the
back door of the house each morning carrying
her starched hat, & ate bacon. On her dresser,
various creams, swabs, a homemade letter holder,
pins. St. Joseph High. St. Anthony (a statue).
The Edmonton General. The Holy

FIELD 6

The boy leans over grey
field. Its breath
whispers
barley, barley, or:
barely. Or
not at all.

The deer's eyes
see aspens,
dark
grey smudge of
lakeshore
oh, down there, apart
from. The boy thinks
of the hospital wall.

He is down by the river now,
wading out to the island.
& pushes the knife
down hard
into the deer.

FIELD 7

The titles were ruined by repetition,
reputation.
They were "field", then "field"
& so on, differentiated by a ciphered
marking, the arabic numbers,
for the sake of

order, which we all love.

We know nothing more about the field
than the one deer in it. Its stomach
full of grain, lying there.

To which will be added, in a few minutes:
the rain.

FIELD 8

The inner narrative we are all proud of.
My father taking the bus to the Lacombe Hospital
to see her, after her graduation.
The graduation, cups of, measurement.
Blue willow, rooted in the water, we say, putting
her hat into the plastic bag, the black stripe pinned to it
Impossible to bend other than this
The two steeples of the hat, curious
dwelling
The stomach of the deer that my brother cut open, now
part of the narrative of the Holy.

FIELD 9

Some mornings she came back
from the Holy
out of snow &
coldness &
no one stopped dreaming

so she ate alone.

Pins, creams, the notes
to the self. The
mirror.

All of our lives, the
Holy, the
hospital she laid in,
came home from,
dressed differently.

Tough willow, we say
Rooted, we say

FIELD 10

It should be more about the field. Already the deer
gapes, my brother's hands pulling out lungs & liver,
the wind is up hard black cloud, the cold guts
with straw stuck to them.
The brother goes off the page, doing something.
The deer television shuts down, its
receptors missing

a few directional stimuli. So
cry if you can.
This is the place for it.
The place where you are all
satisfied.
The deer's torso full of water, hanging
The rain beating the crop down
The end

THE ORIGIN OF HORSES

To imagine the shape of the poem before it occurs, the placement of hieroglyphs on the page, hiero & glyph, sylph & pirouette, the shuddered flank, muscle open in the hoof & shoulder, soft light off white-walled houses, dreamed last night in Spain, just before we drove onto the ferry

The cars had sped off the ramp to make room for us, high beams white hurting. Our camaraderie in the car, us younger than ourselves, as if in high school, & my brother in t-shirt & jeans, appeared suddenly, twenty years old, peaked cap of the Grain Growers shielding his eyes, jumping serious onto the hood of our moving car, then up & into the back seat, top down, not even rushed

breathing.

It was the houses astonished us in Spain, the narrow laneways & cement over hand-made bricks, washed yellow, red tile roofs, busyness; the dog sleeping in the grocery in a bin of clothes, yowling when we woke it. This is Spain, we said to each other, Spain, we're in Spain, the wine-strong smell of the streets & incontestable music on the radio. Sometimes the poem's shape comes of this, three squares thick with wording, & the lone glyph representing the lungs, the icon placed in nearly every poem to honour the lungs' softness. As the brother is honoured, glyph jumping out of nowhere in Spain, dreamed Spain origin of horses in America, the clothes he wore to cut the grass in, in the Rocky Mountains, a symbol of oxygen, the car driven over the shoreline, into the dark of the ferry.

THE BEAUTY OF FURS

At lunch with the girls, the younger ones are talking about furs, & what looks good with certain hair colours. Red fox looks no good with my hair, says one. White fox looks snobbish, beautiful but snobbish, says another one. They talk about the pronunciation of coyote. I think of my brother catching muskrat. I think of pushing the drown-set into the weeds, the freezing water of the Elbow, the brown banks & snow we lived with, soft smell of aspen buds not yet coming out on the trees, & us in our nylon coats in the backyards of Elbow Park Estates, practically downtown, trapping. *Coy-oh-tea*, the women say. In some places they say *Ky-oot* or *Ky-oht*, I say, thinking of the country where my brother now lives, the moan of coyotes unseen, calling the night sky. & me caught in the drown-set so deeply, my breath snuffled for years. & then it comes. They are talking about the beauty of furs, and how so-and-so's family is in the business. I remember, I say, I remember my mother had a muskrat coat, & when she wore it & you grabbed her too hard by the arm, fur came out. Eileen, fifteen years older than me, starts to laugh, & puts her hand on my shoulder, laughing. We both start laughing. I start to explain to her that it was old; my mother wore it to church on Sunday & got upset if we grabbed her arm. We're laughing so hard, now the young ones are looking at us, together we are laughing, in our house there was a beaver coat like that Eileen said, then suddenly we are crying, crying for those fur coats & the pride of our mothers, our mothers' pride, smell of the coat at church on Sunday, smell of the river, & us so small, our hair wet, kneeling in that smell of fur beside our mothers

THE BEAUTY OF FURS: A SITE GLOSSARY

Later you realize it is a poem about being born, the smell of the fur is your mother birthing you & your hair is wet not slicked back but from the wetness of womb, the fur coat the hugest fur of your mother the cunt of your mother from which you have emerged & you cower in this smell The fur coat the sex of women reduced to decoration, & the womb the place of birth becomes the church in which you are standing, the womb reduced to decoration, where women are decoration, where the failure of decoration is the humiliation of women, to wear these coats, these emblems of their own bodies, in church on Sunday, children beside them The church now the place of birth & rebirth, they say *redemption*, everyone knows what this signifies & the mother is trying to pay attention, all the mothers, my mother, & we are children, I am children, a child with wet hair cowlick slicked down perfect, no humiliation, the site still charged with the smell of the river, the coat smell of the river, smell of the birth canal, caught in the drown-set is to be stopped from being born, is to be clenched in the water unable to breathe or see the night sky, the *coyohts* calling me upward, as if in these circumstances, so small beside my mother, I could be born now, but cannot, can I, because we are inside this hugest womb which has already denied us, in which we are decoration, in which men wear dresses & do the cooking, & the slicked hair is not the wet hair of birth but the hair of decoration, as if I could be born now, I am born, my snout warm smelling the wet earth of my mother's fur

SEEBE

The mind's assumptive power
The assumptive power of the mind over the mind
The carrying of spit upward to the mouth on the end of a knife
this incredible spillage,

release of the river behind the dam at Seebe, recoil of water
rushing the gorge, where we have stood, our lines
taut connection between us & the water's surface, our blastular memory,
(t)autological

who we are, now, the spaces between words where time leaks out
& we are finished, finished, gone old;
the table of food finished & the guests left, & the spillage of glasses, &
our shirts empty, empty,

They say what saves the bones is weight-bearing exercise
except for the carrying of children
Which is our namesake,
which is what we do, naming

children,
taking their torsos in & out of the uterine wall
then carrying them, lifting
the weight of the small boy up from the side of the rails
& running forward to the train, stopped for us, his leg soft with blood
spattered my uniform, his leg not broken, just torn a bit at the skin,

This spillage, rusted gates pulled upward
to release the downstream blood
The mind's assumptive power of the Bow at Seebe
Carrying the boy to the conductor & then running back for the
kit, sunlit, "we hit a cow" they said in the lounge car afterward,
& me lifting the boy up from the dam where he was fishing,
the bridge where the whitefish run among the planted trout at Seebe

lifting him upward, his Stoney Indian face & bone weariness, watching me
white woman from the train taking him upward
into the vast, vast emptiness

Actually he was in the weeds
Actually he was nested hurt leg red in the weeds beside the train
so as not to be found again, got that?
All the tourists on the dam fishing sunlit maybe first hot weekend of
summer, delirium, delirium, trout dreams of the uterine memory,
pulled upward on the thin lines, water running high into the reservoir,
oh Bow, oh hotness,

we hit a cow, they said

The sudden yet soft emergency braking, pulling the cars up expert not
too hard, we hit a cow they said in the curved light of the lounge at the
end of it, & breaking out the side door lifting the green box, knowing
nothing, knowing the sunlit heat on the back of the blue uniform,
running down the right of way, the body not used to it yet, this gravelled
running, the hot smell of spruce & light air of curious voices, the boys
on the bridge having run, then; not knowing what would be found
there, thinking of what to do in the bright run in the sun,

1) check breathing if you can find the mouth,
2) stop the bleeding,
3) immobilize fractures,

thinking the second step, going over it in the mind, so that when you
look at someone completely bloody you see blood only where it is
moving, it is the assumptive power of the mind, the mind over the
mind, the deconstructive power of the human body, to take this,
outward

He was in the weeds. & scared. He looked up soft at me. Hey, I say. You're okay. He was hiding there from me. I could see him. & ignored his hiding. Dropped the kit & bent over the torn leg. Bloody, that's all. Only one leg. The foot aligned well with the rest, okay, feeling up & down the bone, no, okay, just torn up & bleeding where? Here. Bleeding here. Okay. Lifting him up then & running carrying him back up to the train, the blue cars creaking, conductor, wait

give him up

& run back, the green kit just sitting tipped on the right of way, beside those weeds, grab it & run back, daring to look around at the trees & warm smell forest finally, jump back into the cars, we're off then

The poem has fallen apart into mere description.
It is years later, thinking of the mind's assumptive power & remembering the train hitting the boy at Seebe, Alberta & how I went out
to get him. Here we have only my assumptions, only the arrogance of Erin Mouré made into the poem; in the course of history, which is description, the boy is mute. We have no way of entering into his images now. The description itself, even if questioned, portrays the arrogance of the author. In all claims to the story, there is muteness. The writer as witness, speaking the stories, is a lie, a liberal bourgeois lie. Because the speech is the writer's speech, and each word of the writer robs the witnessed of their own voice, muting them.

Lifting him up, bone weary, taking him
into the vast, vast emptiness.

ORDER, or RED ENDS

If the order is not certain. The woman in the red cape
lighting a cigarette.
The red end of the cigarette.
What is known, known,
guides us, our tentative hands.
At night, I dream my mouth deep into your body, my hands.
We are looking at each other.
There is a door between us. Our hands touch.

Open.

ORDER 2

To connect for the first time, "this
remarkable love."
The arm entwined with the body, & entwined again,
leaving the fingers. Reflex points for
the sinuses, not the heart.
I test them. We test them.

We like this.

We go on.

ORDER 3

A light scramble over the dance floor
leaves us breathless. The grey shale above,
& over that, the sheer mtn passes.

What we can, or cannot
speak to. We move on.

With our backs turned, you can see
o reader, not what you recalled
of women's beauty, but

ropes, & crampons.

ORDER 4

Don't be afraid of thinking
otherwise. All poems have
their own amazing order,
by which we decode
"the author's intention."
Millions of people get sick of this in Grade 10
& never
read
poetry again.

Later, I tell a group of supervisors that
solving a problem has its ontological aspect,
& is like making a poem.
I read them one by Miklós Radnóti
that starts:
"The moon hangs on a clouded sky.
 I am surprised that I live."

We go on.

Don't make the mistake of thinking this
is poetry. It's not. I just had to say this.
It was in order.
(It is also o.k. to say "ontological"
at this point
in the narrative.)

ORDER 5

If so, this is narrative.

ORDER 6

The problem of our
disobedience.
You are tied to your Catholic upbringing,
X. says.
But Catholicism in Alberta was different, she insisted.
Both ascetic and opulent.
The poor were ascetic and the rich opulent.
We could pass thru the eye of a camel,
or whatever.
I tell you.
We were that insistent, & thin.
The rich, too.
It's enough now.
We remember everything.

ORDER 7

So much influence just ends up
sounding like mockery.
For example: "The red end of the cigarette."
Who said that?

Certain tests can indeed be applied to
the chemical surface of the poem.
Neurasthenic glamour is everywhere, wobbling
on "dude" knees.
But nothing about the author.
Is she a good lay?
Can she kiss?
Who knows.

ORDER 8

This remarkable love. Certain

pressure points of touch, by which
the world is made manifest
to the inner organs, the liver, heart lungs.

It all fits.

The pancreas sees thru a horizontal slat
just over the joint of the thumb, under
the middle fingers.

The feet too. Feet & hands, by which is visible
the internal order.
Red ends of the cable, open

When they touch any being, the
impulse begins

ORDER 9

Sybilline light of the women, dancing
The air bladder of a fish,
turned upward

These comparisons, what we can or
cannot, etc., compare to
At night, remarkable or

hilarious.

Oh, do what you want, friends of mine.
I'm putting my coat on, holding my arms
up over my head, hair, not
with it, having danced in the cigarette smoke,
unable to breathe now, having

had or not had
"a light scramble over the dance floor," or
"two kisses," or should I say
"the eye of a camel," or even
"two beers"

✧ **from** *Sheepish Beauty, Civilian Love*

photon scanner (blue spruce)

HARSH METALLIC (photon)

Extreme sadness of the quail. Quail from the sky, &
otherwise, sad pockets opening up into the sea, such spit, the
sea,

& waking up from this. Small quail in the chest, breathing.
Feathers bunched up in the inner wind, blown clay, the pots
of tiny leaves, thyme or rosemary, fragrance of old bark or
buckskin. On the perches, the small paws of the quail.
Waking up. Dark aisles of silence & bread, *drying bread.*
This, & the quail in the hands, felt suddenly:

the warm river, a trickle, bird wings audible

when the hands move, when they push the torso upward
from the mattress & sheeting
tremulous
its stutter of ligament
connectivity

the breasts still dreaming of a window opened up into the
water the sea & the quail above the mountain townsite
howling beneath the steep green of their outcrop, their
feathers soaked & streaming

(inside the ribcage*
or in memory, beneath the needled tree)

HARSH METALLIC (scanner)

[1]As if we could love, knew how to, our loving

A harsh metallic (blur) (noise)

(a car door shutting)

They stood up out of their chairs

Sudden chairs, warm, deviated or

empty

The noise repeating in the perceptual circuit

Sudden

confusion or agony "the bleat of voices"

The tree normal, the sky normal (blue), the street still

(they are looking)

& sit down again, the room altered, skewed, stereoscope

[2]As if we could love

BANK HILL (photon)

This morning, too, the spit or trickle over
the stones of the hands, in the hands, round stones on which
the feet tremble, crossing the river of spit & haze cut into
burnished blades of light, small cuts in the surface of the
water, surgical
Leading to the straw bank hill on the other side, the mouth
opening up in darkness, the air in the yard (urban)
still
enters into this mouth
dry

the grouse lying under the short pencil marks of the needled
spruce, spruce grouse, thinking "invisible," in-
divisible from the leaves, from the pencil-stroked needles
its bird head & thoughtful eye, leading to the inner circuit
where the watcher sits
upside down in its brain, displaced &
hilarious
hanging from the ground

unreadable*, soles barefoot on the grey slime of those river
stones
Stones of the hand
River in the hand, waking,
moving the lines of the hand upward
The torso raised up
Soaking the room

BANK HILL (scanner)

[1]The asymmetrical gesture of the body, its love

Another being, limbs or limbic

Out of their soft chairs, startled torsos

Crack of air repeated in the inner cortex

The brain aping sudden *car door slammed or*

A still invisible document codifies

identity & recognition

Your left hand under your cloak advises "calm"

Agonic fret of human voices, awaiting

The physical beauty of a remembered touch

An outcry or woman

"doting mad"

[2]The traverse of love, we (scarcely)

INNER MUTINY (photon)

Inner mutiny of the inner quail. The feathers worked up
fissured. A blank space in the asphalt yard & brown grass
appearing. O feathers we have known, will know,
act upon
Our responses governed by the immensity of the
crouched & hidden bird, the hidden quail of spit & stones
we are drinking

as we wake up sudden

this bird in us & the range of action possible, string on its
neck chewed, its leg & paw chewed, its orange paw chewed.
The physical eye. & famous drawer. Or again
above the townsite, the whispered tree & highway noise
deep into the bush, a kind of taiga, the blue trees scribbled
dark
hiding grouse & quail
their eyes

notice

& feathers oiled, it is us wet in the rain the hot drops fallen
& smell of spruce. At last we are here, away from

The body torn out, squelched, is or is not *immortal

*breathing

INNER MUTINY (scanner)

[1]When they lie side by side, the wanton horse (love)

A book slammed shut, the echo

Stood up sudden then resumed their duties "cutting hair"

The third form of possession or madness, of which

poetry

When they lie side by side, recanting

Street invisible smell of sulphur after

Uncodified

The cortical scan repeats the brittle slam of cars

Repeats the known noise, not any explosive power

As resolved by the council of Tiananmen

One year later, his roses

[2]The yearning agonic blister we have known as love

UNICORN EAR (photon)

In the inner cortex, the soft quail with their unicorn ear, &
teardrop, beautiful trembling & soft feet. The orange paws
curled soft against the cage of the rib, the bread's noise
deafens
& she wakes up, vaginally altered, alterity
she has dreamed of, touching the woman's right shoulder
"it's my favourite place to be touched" she speaks back
angry

The dream then vanished under the flower, the fern &
spruce blister sap running, soft eye of the quail
still
watching

"My favourite place" trembles
The wound opened anywhere on the surface map of the body
As it did on his, until the rosary beadwork folded in his
fingers by technicians
The wound mapped anywhere on the surface vaginal of the
chest
& we breathe soft roses
The wound mapped anywhere on the tissue lesions
& we get up daily, we breathe* this bread

UNICORN EAR (scanner)

[1]Bearing her instrument, the wound she so loves

Capable of perfect transmission, or

duty

Stuffed the bird with bread so it can be eaten

Normal, salted

At the table of our sighs where rose petals forget us

The medieval tradition of verse

A harsh crack in the corridor, the door opens

The running figure is a woman crying

The wound on the surface of the body lies

deeper than

[2]To live with fearful(ness) in the name of love

photon scanner 5

BLISTER SPLIT (photon)

Eventually all poems fall into their seam or *gutter*, the
rough trail in the spruce behind the mountain townsite, the
photon blister
split from its scanner, the body (split) from its fertid dis-
continuity of thought, the light freckles of the quail's paws
reach to wipe the hair fallen over the woman's forehead.
Discontinuous,
the voice (stutter) speech is reconstructed in the split across
two hemispheres

"Recognizable speaking" in the photon *here*
& the mute dependency of the right cortex
a stuttered scanner that decodifies or scans
the fifth madness, *over there*

she said, the quail's flutter in the jar of the chest, in which
the lungs' splintered rail, rails of spit broken into wet tissue
(she says) bring up excessive water

What is in excess of the body pissed out or
cut by the pages here, whose binding you must efface
o reader to engage
the hemispheres' simultaneous noise, this *consciousness*
where thought & the body Are one
The bread drying in the corridor
Her grouse-like paws & inner sobbing
puffed up & tree-struck
Capable at last in the neural *tremour, to recognize

*blue spruce

BLISTER SPLIT (scanner)

[1]As if Ideal forms fail to reveal *love*, the hesitant pouring

In any measure, the frivolous hand

Cars in the road, the sudden

Where they stood together, scraping the (forgettable) chair

Does each word bear weight?

If so, what weight.

The cortical circuit unable to identify the noise

To retrieve the words or quail in the woman's fingers

Her "doting madness"

Was it the sound of: *a car door shudder?*

From the oaken dress, the roses tumble

Her lungs seeping where the metal whispered

"The wound now pisses joy"

[2]Her love a trail or *track thru these trees, *indéchiffrable*

*benzene lamp

6 NOTES FOR A MAZURKA

If we are, it is true, without gentleness in our lives
the absolute scent of the haystack
risen from memory
wherein our arms have laboured
this haystack & the yellow smell of it
the dry smell of weeds & limpened grasses
the smell of the motorcycle ridden suddenly
into this hay

If it is true that we are without this gentleness
the strain of the lateral muscles
regulating the spine
the strain of the back, say,
lifting up the bales with work gloves
striped at the wrist
leather palms

hot day

I remember you out there
angry at me

Far behind you   the raked & cut lawn
green
glimmered
a tea party of the empty chairs

2) STRIPED BLUE

Or the work gloves striped blue lying by the door
empty absolute of their fingers the leather palms
greasy in the centre & fingers bent whistling a
famous tune "Have you ever been to Dallas" they
sing crudely & the cows moo they begin to moo
when they hear this having heard of Dallas before
I think on television they press their sides on the
fence-wire "o Dallas is a dreamer" they raise their
lips & moo

3) BURST

The inner noise of the body, string
of the veins & fibrous coatings, muscle
Light glinting off the shoulder, which glistens
white or red or grey
the buds having already burst out on the trees
lilacs
aspens

the yard bright with flowers
& the back bent down
a piano

(As if, beautiful is this
necessary heart strain
the bead of water on the skin
how it got out

from the inside
thru the solid barrier
skin density

it trickled through & formed

they say
visible

4) RUNNER

With a stick or hand your father played that
piano

You yelled & ran

The neighbours closed their windows

The houses were built so close & your yells disturbed
their peaceable dwelling
the planet of their endeavour
maybe their own pianos, someday

You yelled

The piano rang out

5) COWS

Which is why I wonder about the planetary future.
All these people playing pianos of the back
symphonic whistle behind the shoulders
it's a panic
I wonder about it
I wonder about the "panic"
If even the striped gloves are whistling
& the cows howl
& the back's ivories tremble
under the strain of the father's arm

something is fishy
Dexter Gordon is dead
there's no saxophone

Suddenly I realize what silence is
& baffle my ears

The piano keys you wear under your shirt
triumphant

Walking away from me

Yeow

6) "GO IN, NOW"

The inner voice in which we have trembled.
The noise of our fear that is not a tick but a squeezing
of the inner muscle
not a tick but a motion in the blood we mistake for ticking
except those of us
in whom the valve *flutters*
wasting

& who therefore must bow down
& shut up
after the strenuous blow
not looking anywhere

Awaiting the receipt of gentleness
a painstaking clearness

Where the chest & back meet, seamless
("You can go in, now")

A mazurka